# breaking poems

# breaking poems

Suheir Hammad

Cypher Books
New York, New York

Cypher Books
310 Bowery
New York, NY 10012
info@cypherbooks.org / www.cypherbooks.org

Versions of *breaking poems* have appeared in *Al-Raida, Drunken Boat,
Naked Punch, We Begin Here*.  The New World Theater dramatized
some of the poems in *breaking letter(s)*.

ISBN: 978-0-9819131-2-4

book design by Anatole Hernandez

cover image: "Broken"
photo of flower frozen in liquid nitrogen then broken
http://www.flickr.com/photos/dotbenjamin/
ben@benjaminasmith.com

First edition: 2008

The publication of this book was made
possible by a grant from NYSCA

Thank you to The Amherst College Copeland Fellowship, Vona, Hedgebrook, The Palestine Literary Festival and Art Matters for support.

Lisa Simmons and Willie Perdomo, a home for the broken.

Recognize:
The ancestry within me, the elders who raise me, the experience of *Salt of This Sea*, the epiphanies of the Coltranes, the cosmos of Sun Ra, dub, the MCs, poets, painters, singers and musicians breaking throughout, the company of Glen, Zoe, Ralph, Hasan, Sekou, RIP Mahmoud Darwish, the fortitude of the living, my close friends, the lovers, and the haters.  Mojuba.

Those who booked readings and appearances, shared poems, and spread light.  Thank you to the organizers, teachers, artists and activists who are healing the broken in us.

A.G.

My parents and siblings.

One.

dedicated to my sisters

## contents

# breaking poems

## ———— - break - ————

(nyc)

humidity condenses breath

bodies stick and stones gather in a lower back

gray thick moving slow and alone

i am looking for my body

for my form in the foreign
in translation
what am i trying

to say i sit in this body dream
in this body expel
in this body inherit
in this body

here is the poem

i left a long time ago
remember stubble remember unwanted remember touch

i can't remember where i left my body

poem needs form lungs need
air memory needs loss i need
to translate my body because it is profane

what had happened was
i wrote myself out of damage

this is the body of words and spaces
i have found to re-construct

# Suheir Hammad

(deheisha)

my home
girl is there now the air is thick
people don't breathe well hold their
tongues against cursing all of existence
all that would carry on living during this

she wakes to news just the beginning
the same story the one which leaves bodies
behind as tokens of nothing

one family
roasting corn
now all husk
silk
spraying
wind

my home girl's body
would be called white be claimed jewish
is mother and loved by a man who sits in a bay
by telephone and radio and reaches for his lover's body
and finds only formless

she is witness and rage
i pray her body save her
come back with her offer lover a home
daughter a beginning and all of us testimony

the people there tell her they will survive this

if a body can carry through you follow

# breaking poems

(beirut)

a green body obsessed white possessed by all male religion sword
sniper garnishes silicone radishes video radiology vixens eastern
european prostitution manic depression olive oil sweat camps resorts
hair gel all that is life all that is death

the roads and bridges been hit
the airport been hit

where is a body to go

we lived there once my parents sisters and me
i left my skin there still boiling


(tel aviv)

write your own damn poem
build a grammar with something other than bones


(gaza)

a woman's hand cups bloodied sand bits scalp ooze
to the camera and says this is my family


(khan younis)

yamaaaaaaaaa
yamaaaaa


(nyc)

i am waiting for a break
in weather

i am not yet broken

enough to forget
desire but i wish i would

my parents worry i will never marry
i cannot comfort them

(houston)

a family says this is the summer of sacrifice
no vacation no new car no addition to the study
but pedicures and hair relaxing and shape-ups and gyms
mandatory a body must keep up must be presentable

a husband says i wake up and sleep and wake up
and all i think about is gas prices

(bombay)

bomb bay bomb bay bomb bay bomb bay

(exactly brooklyn)

my niece sleeps light
my sister feeds her her body
my clan holds one breath

(new orleans)

there is no wading in this water
a body can be polluted inside and out

# breaking poems

(baghdad)

the children watch from bodies roasting by roadsides
they fall in love with the soldiers killing them
they see soldiers are bodies with orders
they wish for something to follow

a star an idea called hope sick as it sounds


(here)

is my body

is my body
an offering to give or to receive

wait for storm
know that even this is not it
that when it comes
break will be fire baptism
and in the ashes there
is my body

# Suheir Hammad

## ——————— - (wind) break (her) - ———————

fairuz turquoise dawn ears ring
voice diwan detroit divine
smoke full lips fall on back baalbek
museum mezze sabra jordan black
june in jerusualem

bi albek
almonds coffee darwish
the eighties the ground the zeroes
tabla in brooklyn air so thick beat hung there
hips reflected the breath someone was drumming
to accompany the dying and the living
somewhere far and somewhere close

a sweeping
   find shelter in a cross
a reckoning
   find none at all
people looking to be seen
   even if the last moments
even if after life

last fall her birthday
i ask my homegirl what she wants
bi albek
she leaps to fall in love
i offer earrings and we kiss the beirut
sky color of bruised healing

kiss it born
kiss it ill
kiss it youth
kiss it prison
kiss it collective
kiss it punishment
kiss it viral
kiss it infected
kiss it missing

# breaking poems

kiss it childhood
kiss it water
kiss it dignity
kiss it burning
kiss it alone
kiss it so alone
kiss it kiss it

habibi wants the moon
but the moon is far away

a city in exile

bi albe ana nar

curl of flame jeweled arms
flash smile flash flesh perfect cut damage tapestry vintage
design with no weapons dress to kill it means you don't die
from the powerlessness of it
from the leap to fall in love
from believing in rebuilding

# Suheir Hammad

## ———— - break (still) - ————

between pyramids
white feather
nestled in hair flammable

recognize the buffalo

not minimalism this
shit is destruction
of language is adonis
adnan lament is elmaz heart
wails shattered is a shot
in the face
as the enemy comes
into your heart and sets
up walls and sets a drama
the first civil war is there

and always happening
in june's living room

> the children who can't run are the charred dead
> privilege will not save it is the noose
> people get off on this shit they must

beirut is still sexier than gaza
gaza is still closer than sudan
sudan still iraq still
you your own civil war still

# breaking poems

yo thunder gun clap flash flood warning

cumin kizbara a kiss bara
herb quartz strung key feather door
internet iced letters coffee clove guinness beats
beats beats july heat miriam medicine
what you become not just on paper
beautiful bosom in love beirut

corner the corniche
stop lean against
a railing wave foreigners goodbye
turn and walk into a bomb

we no longer know language

asunder sun dare ash judge warring

ribs borders razors geneva guava evacuate demonstrate
against blinding
emperor's mission religion

cane wa able
the first civil war still raging

humiliate a people distract the rest

trademark star brand dreams seeds
water new world old words
this ain't living

words are against us
there is a math only subtracts

# Suheir Hammad

## ———— - break (bas) - ————

bas
bastana
ana bastana
bas

daily papers photo babies
charred bread no life

venus chaired motionless shaking
bleeds currents

astonished stars cry

bas

gather armless
gather heart broke
gather just broke
gather harvest
gather blood
gather thirst

ride moon bare
back through night
conjure lion stretch
sunrise reaching raw ankles

bas ana

image mirage libnan woman khadra
khalas last call rouged up bought
down maze mezze liquor
rich sweat raw flesh mint civil
warm family foreign faded
coast defiant jaded
jupiter altar smote cypress
loudest crescent siren

# breaking poems

occupier vampire
tell like is

gather orphaned
gather barren
gather limbs
gather touch
gather eye light
gather close
realize

bastana ana alone
bas not

# Suheir Hammad

## ———— - break (clustered) - ————

all holy history banned
unwritten books predicted the past
projected future but my head
unwraps around what appears
limitless man's creative violence

whose son will it be
which male child will perish
a new day

our boys' deaths galvanize
we cherish corpses

we mourn women complicated
bitches get beat daily

profits made
prophets ignored

worn tooth enamel salted lemon childhoods

all colors run
none of us solid

don't look for shadow
behind me i carry it within

i live cycles of light and darkness
rhythm is half silence
i see now
i never was one
and not the other
sickness health tender violence

i think now i never was
pure before form
i was storm blind
ignorant still am

# breaking poems

humanity contracted itself
blind malignant i
never was pure

girls spoiled before ripened
language can't math me
i experience exponentially
everything is
everything

one woman loses 15 maybe 20 members of her family
one woman loses 6
one woman loses her head
one woman searches rubble
one woman feeds on trash
one woman shoots her face
one woman shoots her husband
one woman straps herself
one woman gives birth to a baby
one woman gives birth to borders
one woman no longer believes love will ever find her
one woman never did

where do refugee hearts go
broken dissed placed
where they're not from
don't want to be
missed faced with absence

we mourn each one
or we mean nothing at all

my spine curves spiral
precipice running to and running
from humans beings

cluster bombs left behind
de-facto land mines
a smoldering grief

harvest contaminated tobacco
harvest bombs
harvest baby teeth
harvest palms
smoke
harvest witness
smoke
salvation
smoke
resolutions
smoke
redemption
smoke

breathe

do not fear what has blown up
if you must fear
the un-exploded

# breaking poems

view our lives through
the prism hurricane

check what   got flooded
check what   salt preserved
check what   wind kissed

you feeling me

see how we waded
see how we waited

monarchs danced around us

muttered lies
murdered in fives
and tens and twenties

we age gracefully
our youth burns

we rhyme of rivers
swim in vernacular

forced paths irrigated soil
migrated bloodlines coiled
around our aching spines

stereo our lives
through sonic boom

check how we crunk
check how we dip
check how we slide

we loud and muted

you hear me

powerless we take death
into our own hands
gold plate our teeth
we crypt dance

yes we were sold dreams
still we bought them
here the receipt

we escaped
goaded

we marked and tatted

we never mattered

feel me

we near
washed away
almost bombed out

brass rings us

exploded melody

the rushing
of our flesh
we complex sun
resented complexion

life is court enough
god is witness

hear me
feel me
kiss this

# breaking poems

cross legs cross back cross self

marie mary mariam
our golden ladies

maria weeping

women in hats   women in veils   women in crowns
beheaded women   braided women   dyed women

miriam sleeps alone   aches for touch   kisses lipstick
marie sleeps around   longs for bond   mirrored face
mary does not sleep   wants child   bears herself
maria weeping

yamma il amar al bab
sun through window

yamma we in need of fellowship
our hearts do not trust
men yamma our hearts
do not trust themselves yamma

yeah   we polish pain   glitter it
wash flooded feet   frizz hair
offer flesh to hungered   dizzy
quartered   watered

slummed and sexed
we collect swords
knives spears arrows guns missiles pipes

we handle them bare handed   long time
we love them shiney

we look up   from the bottom
of hearts   we pray on knees   trying to live

# Suheir Hammad

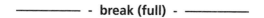

## - break (full) -

wolf visits her dream
licks where the poem
punctures skin
whistles mississippi into her
back bones her
hums a psalm
from upper room

dear god
she miss her dead

dear god everyone she ever love
seen same moon
framed by nar
escape

saturn returned the beautiful
visits her in water
paints her muse
fixes fairuz in morning
um kolthom at night
gazes her awake

wolf and beautiful and all
whose songs she sings

dear god
a woman singing somewhere tight
shoes off toes stretching push
up flesh tone mascara lined lips
almonds smoking hearts

so much love
a living soul
a moon full

# breaking poems

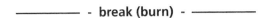

————— - **break (burn)** - —————

oh
ana see now
ana unraveling

all the collected
like wind in my hands
woven   ribbons   now smoke   oh

ana now storming
bringing nar

heart
entangled

this is growth
or death
or both

dear god   one body   inherited two minds all time   one shelters
cellular belief in something love   another must not believe   cannot
believe i am worth   proof this smoldering   the balance madness

i have thrown out the flowers
i have blown out the candle
i have offered my flesh
i have kissed lips flaming
i have kissed myself away

oh
ana the blazing

trailing road

dear god   i am burning   fingers embers   feathers shed

dear god   i am changing   so are you

# Suheir Hammad

all matter related
we connected

ana on corners
holy grams
ana incarcerated light

gaze me

ana gaza
you can't see me

ana blood wa memory

it was all a dream
lion kissing me

ana harb
heart
ana har

ana wa ana
we related
woven
ultimate design
physical dream

please excuse my state of disappearance
been renovating structure
innovating space
hype earrings on

# breaking poems

## ———— - break (layla bye) - ————

oya gathers orphans wa sweeps cemeteries wa wars
oya un-waxed wa spinning
om kolthom fairuz nina ana spinning

the woman singing

is lock down
broke key
singing off
translinear light

hiya pinwheel
hiya hurricane ain't over
hiya singing

> habibi sleeps on the color of my lips
> is lion roaming away
> habibi kan in khan younis
> kan in captain's cabin
> kan on hot corners
> kan in brooklyn
> habibi can chant lovely
> make the best coffee
> wa drum
> wa dream
> wa draw me
>
> habibi bido il amar
> habibi ibn il nar
>
> ya habibi
> when oh

the woman
broke lock
singing off key
oya tornado
translinear me

# Suheir Hammad

## ———————— - break (shape) - ————————

shifting
gathering
formation to break

dahlias giving ghost

life is sad bas beautiful
discordant melody chaotic
harmony a woman giving head
wa heart wa flesh

quantum

in qana eyes exploded wa vehicles wa children wa bisas

bas

rendering wa detention wa rendition wa redemption marginal scarab
scurrred broken arabic bonded trumpet hearted spinning word

bas

baalbek sunset
fairuz through cedar
licorice liquor wa raw meat
sweated mint wa sore hands
war behind wa ahead

in gaza still flesh is ashed
wa smoked wa denied
a woman's chest caves in
smoke escapes legs

i was dreaming when i wrote this
habibi's prayers in my hands
i held his rhythm bi albe
he held me an instrument
an iridescent note

# breaking poems

## ———— - break (waxing) - ————

fort de trois motor city dilla belle isle lebanese sweet exhaust forked
roads wa spooned lovers wa tupac mowed down motown memory

break your self
ful
nana
wa khobz wa zaatar wa zeit

under sky navel gazing stars
orange groved music yasmine jenin city jenin girl
un deux trois soleils rai amar waxing sun ra
tabla dome tac-teek static sniper roof shambhala
mandala of broken hearts twirls depleted geranium

bastana full moon

dear god ana hawa
wa oil in lamp
light out desert
ana garden wa growth
seed self wa flower
wa tendered

nana w'ameen

# Suheir Hammad

## ———————— - break (maktoub) - ————————

moon
same in ramallah wa new orleans wa jerusalem wa johannesburg wa
beirut same moon

body responds lunarly
a pulling
in time a tearing
out time a warda blooming

ana garden

ana love destroyed cities wa broken fathers distant
lovers silent brothers
same moon

water
paper wa books wa laws wa swears wa promises wa resolutions wa
history
vulnerable to flood
water same moon

ana ocean

nar
bellies wa tires wa homes wa jails wa shoes wa bridges wa desks wa
wara flammable nar wa water wa moon

the order is dis
then that
luna tidal ever shifting ana changing
gaza worrying ya allah
destined to change
same moon
go through changes
same moon

# breaking poems

jesus left at thirty three

full saturn revolution returning messiah

math a myth wa language a lie

scorpio sun wa libra amar

yo this beat nar yo
nod head right off blow up spot wa kill crowd wa
bomb walls break dance wa break off grilled face
iced teeth wa break me sick ill music sickle
self amnesia

ana gathering selves into new
city under construction gaza eyes pitted zeitoun spit meat taqasim
brooklyn broken english wa exiled arabs sampled

> i start to blink and then i think
> reality paper my thoughts the ink
> what i'm writing is strapped in between these lines
> i'll exist when i out run time

ana sawah wa thousand wa one nights wa ahwak
morning ahwa boiling resurrection no sugar no touch

habibi writ his name in water
rhymed sixteen bars wa sang mawal blue heavy brass hair
wool wa ana still waiting missing messiah zei self missing my

habibi don't see me
he gaze stars of different flame

# Suheir Hammad

i left at thirty three
thirty three shots from twin clocks
yo sixteen apiece equal thirty two
that means one of god's suns was holding seventeen
twenty seven hit my saturn dream
six went into me
everybody gotta be born sometime

my eyes burn phosphorous darkened angels broke wings no touch no
touch so much language clustered so much damage cluttered morgue
drawers baby corpses combust when exposed to air in gaza doctors
open bombed bodies find organs on fire wa these people still alive the
dead their wounds flame after spirit gone

fluorescent gardens tended by pyromaniacal men
ana warda exploded tears come busting me open cranial guitar
strumming me a psalm my palms stigmatized heart white butterflies
expand lungs wa bastana new vision same old same sold humanity

somebody touch me jesus

# breaking poems

────────── - break (balance) - ──────────

everything is

looking for balance
in my body

this the thing

everything
once broke open deluge original
ark naked fallen stars

ana beside river myself
humble prayers broke
pity please don't become me

way poet starts poem
in full moon
in box empty
waving for a call
a soweto sunset

space habibi in head wa heart
not math space in daily

at dawn reach for ra wa kiss sky

my homegirl's morning counting gaza bodies
she will tell you the dead do not kiss
wa curly hair needs tending

no remainder melting dice craps all gamble tipping
point internal compass wa complicit wa content wa violent

way poem ends poem

# Suheir Hammad

## ———— - break (for love) - ————

heavy breathing drum machines

west banked sisters hold each curly heads ducked ducked loose
bullets tight soldiers loz eyed oranges in blood explosion of hair

the weary shoulder sacred
the pulsing wrist sacred
the clasped hand temple
the smoking chest temple
sister holy fly sister holy

terra material prima wa ana lapis azure flame wa scarlet star ana mud wa
huddled into shelters wa centers off balance bastana vision wa epiphany

zooted wa cased
air yo dynamic
w'ana mashi layale
drum skin stretched far

ya rayah when my sapphire dusted dream static supreme

dream
crash bombs everyone around me
dream
sash green gold coins surround me
dream
flash dear god flood within me

tremor moon seas moan treble please sing trouble keys

# breaking poems

## - break (water) -

abu-dis missing sunrise
abu-dis missing sunset

ground cipher groundless isis stretch searches pieces

my body upon cutting open
look for the broken bits
the aimless
leave them as found
wa finally leave a scar

trust only stars habibi a mirage a gold tree on chain spark trees on lips
smoke hawa over sunrise hennessy under pillow batata okra dawn
clave iron clove fist silver oasis oriki bata cinnamon offering ana
break into language insurgent

zam zam in desert
hagar springs isis remembers mary reaps
woman looking for body i think she is coming
the feminine in all i think she is coming
rain tears mist seas i think she is coming

# Suheir Hammad

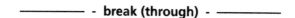

## ─────── - break (through) - ───────

red wa black feathered ears girdle wasted girl
explosive abdomen damaged holy gram

malcolm midnight baldwin dawn unseasoned weather
homegirls nesting opening blossom chest bear to love despite all

what you got
to kill in order
to leave home
bridges over
head ankles aflame

what you got to kill in order to live

sometimes i leave my body wa i
leave my country wa my religion
sometimes leaving is my religion

pray with me habibi
wa over wa within

# breaking poems

─────── - break (clean) - ───────

dawn sky midnight long past lightening dusk rose horizon

sunrise zam zam coffee suzan w'ana healing swell then bruise then
harden cuts heal like hearts please god this hurt do not calcify
endurance half faith

heal clean

al waha ahead snake heart in purse anti-venom
wa own heart in fist against breaking

radio reports growing exodus west bank life no future
how many times can you refugee

wonder land alice coltrane organ raga brooklyn babka home boy

break meta morpheus
break don't lead ending
break new dream

w'allah even in war women cry over hearts broken
wa even in privilege women want
wa injury dynamic
wa each hurt sings own song

god bless the non-violent
ooooh god bless them

# Suheir Hammad

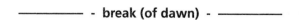

## ———— - break (of dawn) - ————

love zei dam zei water
left running teeth brushing wa washing
beer glasses wa ahwa mugs american showers jets fuel
streams fading river oloukun palace atlantis
wasted easy like this

zei ill hawa ana searching for my body carried in
wind wa writ in water

gaza visa denied no beit hanoun tutu

omi tutu flaming heart
omi tutu burning earth

checkpoints roadblocks hot blocks cellblocks awed wa shocked
bitches bleed daily

when the moon visits
kiss her back kiss her knees kiss her feet
chest heavy kiss through heart

fold sky into skirt must be full stone wash moon light dry clean
wounds pinup dreams gather fabrications adorn breath a dress life jade
wa hematite olive wood beads waisted elaborated hum rumi
seen ha ya ra embroidered horizon

women bury family in earth wa rage in earth wa darken face with
earth water rising borders dissolving walls will break money will
break control will break heart will break easy like this habibi like this

# breaking poems

(here)

is the poem

isis was remembering herself
all that travel all that ache

i confuse spirit wa flesh
especially in dark

seen

what had happened was nation wa honor wa religion wa language
all that shaped me was illusion formless

post surgery stretch isis stitching wa searching for her body


(jerusalem)

habibi smokes cigayer in his grave awaiting resurrection


(baghdad)

if thieves see your beauty they will loot
some think they liberators wa some saviors
wa ooohh girl a few will even love you

long the way


(new jerusalem)

when he says he's not the one believe him
act like you now

(here)

is the poem
lived in one fractured body
a relic of war
ana no one's soldier
khalas
ana no one's instrument
ana own music
ana own muse
khalas all this breaking

# breaking poems

## — - break (wave) - —

here is the thing
the poem is the body

i misplaced it

oceanic void refracted shallow land locked
heart reflected bodies of water

love wa ocean well up within

the break collapsing a cross plunging wa surging
crest don't fully break bas bottom steepens wa caves
in caverns fathomless
all ever seen of me is foam

water floats bodies wa flows poems zei women

here is the thing
the body is the poem

placed in habibi's mouth
placed in men's hands
placed on maps wa within lines wa between covers

ana all this time
translating waves into language bas missing
what i had wanted to say was

# Suheir Hammad

———— - **break (transition)** - ————

there is no body
no matter

i gave it away wila it was taken w'allah what i had
what i had wanted to say was

w'allah if someone touches me
i will break open sesame abracadabra arab cadavers posted
on net spun out bottles sashes wa ashes musk wa dusk

once there was path here habibi
once there was road

i wail here
i wait there

for my body a break a kiss god the last
dance of the night i know nothing i wait
for break of dawn open doors clear roads un-manned time

ana in transit ion

i left my body somewhere
i remember rooms
bas i don't remember walls

# breaking poems

something in me is dying it is brilliant
and the thing is who i used to be it is
walking beside me wa
ribbon adorning broken
neck kiss me on my broken
back kiss me on my broken
body collapse into water
into demolished homes into fire
into bulldozed girls into air into thought
into body into wall collapsing onto itself

live life off the wall my people live life off the wall

did i say something i meant everything

# Suheir Hammad

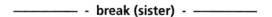

## - break (sister) -

ramallah is closed
zei a heart shuttered wa fortified
bas inside a waiting a held
breath

gaza is on fire
zei a heart feeding on itself
so hungry mistaking
flame for warmth

cities wa women die like this habibi
wa cities wa women live

# breaking poems

## —————— - break (naher el bared) - ——————

cool river burning

ana threading wounded knee
salt water breaking

a planet is my body a higher glyph
habibi's sphinx lips on nile back
shabab drum face jaded
stoned eyes domed wa hooded

hathor moon blood letting
refugees rewind exile

poem is my body my language my country
wa bas ana closed to tourism
ana closed to journalists wa bas
ana closed to translation

## ———— - break (heads) - ————

bad ass boys gather genes pockets of 45s wa m16s
gift me jabal harvest steel
shells spent childhoods pop seeds crack
teeth braced wa jailed word bond
walled bombed witness
bribed wire testimony between
razors babies raised wa dresses
caught a body torn factioned out fitted
woman on the rocks straight up against wall

ghost on pier

the demolished is haunted wa the stolen
ma forget bas i can't remember
the way back to ahead

# breaking poems

**———— - break (me) - ————**

ana my language always broken all
ways lost ana my language wa
i miss my people

# Suheir Hammad

## ———— - break (is this) - ————

habibi got this complex occupation

nine lyric nines i carry him poetry that's a part of me
sit at a tension checked wa pointed interned direction myrrh smoked
mirror scent rose water all ever saved me was a token a ghetto loop
some hood hoop earrings rolled up bless sweat our lady of everything
is everything

jinn on ice calm cante moro throated nefertiti bust ogun iron skirted
past half time quarter noted collect calls new york upstate of
emergency mind the gap between genesis and now one time for those
ain't here my brothers ready to die coming out of ancient queens
bridged to future space afro asiatic astro destiny maktoub it's mine it's
mine it's mine exu born into a theft disarmed weapons communicate
bodies dispersed forever urban

isis hid herself in pharaoh's torso ana hide self in habibi's gypsy song
accorded notes wa plaited tones wa we still looking for our world

# breaking poems

———————— - break ( construction) paper  - ——————

hy gaza can die so easy in front of every one and no one say no gaza
 maze gaza as haze of nonhumans wa generalized attacks militant
opulation no such thing as civilian

alculate torture justified sophisticated even gauzed eyes belted necks
osed teeth begging mercenaries off backs begging mercenaries off
aughters impossible imagine this that everyday some kind of peace
 keeping quiet

he many moons of a life night a time

ne feels it in every way the disconnect
he lack the rush the din the break in the words in the rubble in
he numbers the numbers were folk fog morning the nothing
he pinched back summer ends the bombing don't other people's
fetimes play noise in back ground upturned wa planted the nothing
ways within broken a handful of shards mostly some wa how i learned
uttoned consent open internal design combustion phoenix civil
his course war an aesthetic body as assemblage

# Suheir Hammad

## - break (embargo) -

between us wall wara wall wa ana i ain't jinn wa ana i
ain't phoenix between us yama walls ya allah first wa last
within me breaking sunset over into canaan way dawn
into egypt river running through women carry their men
framed cornered memorial el umma say ameen cigarettes
fuel gaza kemet crossing fingers one hand birds one flock

the dream after the dream
alone fisherman grandfather's sea

gaza pouring exodus resonant alien smoked out blunted absolute
cipher grace pepper calligraphy hunted cartoonist hunted doctor
hunted moderate hunted righteous hunted baba haunted

some people excavate what they love like looted pyramid empty
stomach worried bead browse these streets carbon 14
proportioned formless dark hidden water

habibi chant soul first soul fist sought fashioned criminal gazelle
leaping fence habibi chant down walls with song with song i reach for

# breaking poems

—————  - **break (memories don't live like people do)** -  —————


mallah rooster outside hot rock hard times threw up too
uch everything beautiful wa occupied terra amped wired bound
awked spread regal bearing taj exploding cinnamon sticks wa fire
ext translocation trans-jordan borders passes wa ports transliterated
rabic illiterate scripted heavy crested embroidered stitched steady
ested

on't tell me you know this lonely

ather brother missing husband remember father birth dreaming
re-set rewind pre-crime was there ever there a peace was habibi ever
ere were
ny people ever free was there a way out of this forever was a mustard
eed my faith yellow canary in gold skirt shift mind it was always a
egular day
normal day a ordinary day when i stop to think clear a sky before

# Suheir Hammad

## ——————— - break (history) - ———————

over head bring all your dead living splits throat singing break opens
hoarded land splintered hand maiden how long you gonna call me
militant what is the mathematics of today what sekou say a ring
spinning phoenix as singed dove is street pigeon as chicken head is
hawked bird roland kirk codes survive mingus in the ganges haitians
ghost guantanamo jericho sycamore trumpet tell el sultan lost you
never know the well within the wall the swell of him the wave
the wail within the dam in kin the wall
the wall the echo within

# breaking poems

ulture lacking carnival always war lord a mercy lunacy
what mean crazy commander chief say sky red wa people swallow
indigo wa oil wa lower ninth flooding wa melted sky scraping throat
ward raw wave burning mothers of children who are fish

lues print body as nation costume as custom taxed
adornment oriental ornament indian lining

na min a clan destined grounded under ironed fisted manifested upon
horned women crowned men crowded streets paths to ruin scorned
girls proud boys

abibi the sun a preacher the moon a crescent medina groom nightly
visit  monthly  cycle  endless  tour  abandoned  site  drowned  yaffa
xtinguished tiles geometric design hemming in sons swept into night
anks swim in dreams of no horizon

na gathering cinnamon sticks to nest a burning always the
phoenix the pigeons the doves on urban ledge wa head braced
its wall wa always in no end no sight

# Suheir Hammad

## ———— - break (face) - ————

qalandia a head a family four so quiet their absence alert walk forwar
away permission denied hospital slip a father blind thigh iv hand son
shoulder boy what 4 who 5 the mother holds a baby low whimper i
blanket nonviolence is another's dream a haunting map projected ont
body a memory where men done what they been a blueprint of fligh
sun of spare parts of wet lands open women sea loss waves voice
bass mirror my face the road map the pieces plan the partition through

# breaking poems

rst  brush  gravity  silver  combed  crescent  twist  recently  ancient
itness ages sight misted weighed sin water bone sift dust iron molted
rgan  music  brass  bayou  sunlit  fabric  barely  seamed  loosened chalice
rch encoded ana all come me hallowed cheeks carved river knees
roken  hymn  paradise  street  dime  mined  iced  conned  toured  base
avel shadow current sea gilded bent whore eyes on stunned set face

# breaking poems

*ahwa:* coffee
*ahwak:* a longing more than words
*abdel halim:* song
*amar* : moon / *yamma il amar al bab* from a fairuz song
*ana:* me / i
*bab:* door
*bas:* stop / enough / just
*bastana:* i wait
*bi albe / albek:* in my / your heart (fem)
*bido:* he wants
*bisas:* cats
*dam:* blood
*ful* : fava beans
*habibi:* beloved / my love
*har:* heat
*harb:* war
*hawa:* wind / love / longing
*hiya:* she is
*ibn:* son
*jabal:* hill
*kan:* was
*khadra:* green (fem)
*khalas:* no more
*khobz:* bread
*loz:* almonds
*ma:* not
*min:* from
*nana:* mint
*nar:* fire
*omi tutu yoruba:* cool water
*sawah:* traveler / abdel halim hafiz song
*shabab:* brothers / young men
*umma:* the people
*w'ana mashi layale:* and i am walking nights / nightly
*wa:* and / also half of boo boo (ex. mama, i got a wawa wa it hurt)
*waha:* oasis
*warda:* flower
*ya rayah:* he who leaves / travels / folk song
*yamma:* mama
*zei:* like
*zeit:* oil

# Suheir Hammad

breaking poems in the chronological order they were written.
a love supreme got me over wa through breaks.
john coltrane's masterpiece offered acknowledgement, resolution,
pursuance, psalm.  no resolution at the end.  there is no end.
alpha.  alef.  most high.
humble this offering.  wa thankful.


thank you to the people and elements of new orleans, detroit,
kingston, london, paris, soweto, beirut, cairo, johannesburg, st.
mary's, amherst, oakland, bahia de salvador, olympia, los angeles,
berlin, marseilles, brooklyn wa all of palestine, where these poems
were dreamt, lived wa written.

## About the Author

Suheir Hammad's books are *Born Palestinian, Born Black*, *Drops of This Story* and *ZaatarDiva*. Her award winning work has appeared in many journals and anthologies, as well as on stage in the TONY Award winning, *Russell Simmons Presents Def Poetry Jam on Broadway*, and on HBO in the Peabody Award winning original series of the same name. The NY Hip-Hop Theater Festival and the New World Theater have produced her works, *Blood Trinity* and *breaking letter(s)*. Narrator of the documentary, *The Fourth World War*, her poetry has appeared on DJ K-Salaam's albums. She appears in the Cannes Film Festival 2008 "Un Certain Regard" official selection feature, *Salt of This Sea*. Recipient of a Copeland Fellowship and a Sister of Fire honor, Suheir has read her work in many cities around the world.